HOW TO ANALYZE PEOPLE

The simple guide to quickly read people's
and see if they are lying to you.

Oliver Bennet

Table of Contents – How to analyze people

Chapter 1:   Golden Rules for Analyzing People

It is so easy to get things wrong when analyzing people. What you see, the nonverbal cues, might mean and translate differently from what you think. Reading body language is more than the basic gestures. To avoid making wrong assumptions, these three golden rules will help mold your skills.

Don't Read Individual Gestures

Here's one of the first mistakes you can make when analyzing people. It is often wrong to analyze gestures individually. Most times, individual gestures usually have no meaning and are inconsequential to the overall body language of the person you want to analyze.

Like verbal languages, body languages come with all the rudiments of grammar—words, punctuation, and sentences. Each gesture is like a word, and as we all know, a word can have a myriad of definitions. For example, scratching the head comes with lots of meaning—dandruff, forgetfulness, lying, or just a childhood habit. Perhaps the subject's mother may have patted his head a lot during childhood, and the habit stuck as he or she grew up.

Therefore, it is only until you put the individual gestures (words) into clusters (sentences), that you will reveal the truth about the person's feelings. Never forget that you need to have a cluster of body languages before you can accurately analyze people.

Let's examine a body language cluster of someone interested in what you are saying to support our point on clusters. Imagine you are sitting across an interviewer whose body language exhibits the hand-to-face gesture. This body language involves sitting with your legs crossed (defensive position), your index finger pointing up the cheeks, your thumbs supporting the chin, and another finger covering the mouth.

When you combine these individual gestures to form a body language cluster, you can safely conclude that the interviewer doesn't like what they are hearing. What's more? The cross-legged position shows that he or she is holding back negative feelings. At this point, you should know that there's little chance of winning over the person.

Search for Harmony

Do you remember the phrase "Actions speak louder than words?" Yes, your actions speak about ten times louder than your words. Therefore, when your body language is not consistent with what you say, conscious people, are likely to spot the discrepancy.

Let's go back to the example in the first rule. If you were to ask the interviewer to give an opinion on what you said earlier and he replied that he disagreed with you, his body language will correlate with his verbal statement. In other words, his body language is in harmony with his verbal sentences. However, if he said he agreed with what you said, there's a high chance that he's lying since his body language is not in harmony with his words. And that is one of the steps in detecting a lie.

Why don't we look at another scenario before we proceed to the next rule? Suppose a speaker is standing on a stage, speaking confidently with his arms crossed (defensive position) and his chin pointing toward his chest (hostile position). In this position, if the speaker is telling us about how open and receptive, he is to new ideas, would you believe him? What if he tries to assure you of his caring and gentle nature with his fists clenched and repeatedly hitting the lectern? By observing the disharmony between his verbal sentences and his body language, you will detect that he is insincere.

Read Gestures in Context

What would you think of when you see someone sitting at a park with his chin down, and legs and arms crossed? You might probably say he is being defensive and being insincere. Well, congrats, since you now understand how to read body language clusters.

But wait a minute! Before we put the final stamp on your conclusions, why don't you observe the environment's gestures? What if it was a cold and windy day and the subject was trying to shield himself from the elements? So, when you take the environment and circumstance into consideration, you will create an accurate analysis of people. What if the subject assumed the same position in a library? Then you can safely assume that the subject is being defensive.

Recognize and Decipher Quirky Nonverbal Cues

There are universal body languages that are not specific to a group of people. These universal signals are easy to detect and analyze. You should know that there is a second type of nonverbal signal that's limited to an individual. This is referred to as a quirky nonverbal cue.

Mind you, these less popular signals are hard to detect and are often associated with behavioral patterns formed out of habit. To detect quirky nonverbal cues, you have to search for behavioral patterns in the people you interact with frequently. It's hard to detect these with those you are meeting for the first time. The more you interact with someone, the better your chances of discovering that behavioral pattern upon which you would base your analysis.

For instance, if a colleague always scratches his nose and bites his lips before going into your boss's office, it might be a reliable quirky nonverbal cue that speaks of his nervousness. Undoubtedly, these nonverbal cues have become his gestures to show how nervous or flustered he is.

Try to Establish Baseline Behaviors

Establishing a base behavior is a critical rule in analyzing people. When you interact with people in your workplace, parties, hangouts, or family gatherings, try to grip on their baseline behavior. In simpler terms, try to understand their normal phase—how they act without any pressure or external stimuli.

Start by studying their normal sitting posture, their feet' usual position, their common facial expression, their posture, and the tilt of their head, where they place their personal belongings, and so many other nonverbal tics. Mind you, this is not for you to start acting all creepy around those you interact with, or else they will tense up around you.

The goal is to know how to differentiate their "normal" face and stressed-out face. This rule is not limited to those you are familiar with; you can also apply it to strangers. At the start of your interaction, you should note the "starting point." Establishing a "starting point" or baseline will help you gauge if the person has deviated from it.

Study Behavioral Changes That Could Lead a Change in Decision

Let's paint a scenario: You have been working on a deal for quite a long time, and you've finally gotten the invite to pitch your ideas to a company's executive. A few minutes into the meeting, you start receiving positive vibes from the executive. "This is already a success," you tell yourself. However, the boss receives a call just before he makes his final decision. While on the call, you noticed a difference in his mood.

You observed a change in his body language from being receptive to defensive. At this point, the signal you are getting from the company executive is called an intention cue. These are signals that reveal what a person is about to do, and it gives the observer the time to act fast.

Watch Out for Misleading Nonverbal Clues

You will undoubtedly come across fake or misleading nonverbal clues in the course of analyzing people—it's unavoidable. It takes a lot of experience and practice to differentiate between real nonverbal clues and counterfeits.

Veteran readers can also fail to spot the difference between the two. Therefore, you need to carefully observe before making your judgments.

Distinguish Between Comfort and Discomfort

Let's face it, there are many nonverbal signs to watch out for. The list is endless, and it might lead to confusion if you try to actively look for them all. Therefore, I've created a trick for you to easily detect and understand the nonverbal language you are dealing with.

When in doubt in evaluating a body language signal, all you have to do is ask yourself if it looks like a comfort behavior, such as happiness or contentment, or if it looks like a discomfort behavior, such as unhappiness, stress, anxiety, or disappointment. Most of the instances, you will be able to place nonverbal signals into these two main categories.

Don't Act Like a Creep When Analyzing People

Nonverbal language enables you to assess people and decode their emotions accurately. One thing you should avoid is making it noticeable that you are observing people. Observe with subtlety.

Most folks tend to stare at people when they first try to read on their emotions and thoughts. Analyzing people aims to analyze them unobtrusively because people tend to clam up and restrict their body language when they notice an intense stare. So, work on perfecting your observation skills, and you can get to that point where your efforts will be subtle and successful. Remember, it's all about persistence and practice.

So Why Do You Misread?

Remember, it is possible to make mistakes when you read people. Many body language books teach you that someone has a weak character if he has a weak or limp handshake. But ask yourself this: what if the person is suffering from arthritis or any ailment that might affect his hand grip? What about artists, sculptors, surgeons, and therapists who rely on their hands' perfect condition to get their work done? These people might prefer giving you a weak handshake to prevent unnecessary damage to their hands.

When it comes to analyzing people, there are many factors involved that people might often overlook in a bid to act as the next Sherlock Holmes. Tight-fitting clothes might restrict some people's ability to exhibit certain body language. For instance, ladies with short skirts often have to keep their legs closed, making them less approachable. Although these circumstances only apply to a minority, it is important to consider the effects of a person's physical restrictions on their body language.

So, if it is possible to misread body language, can people also fake it? This is where I set the facts straight; you can't fake body language. Your body will always betray you to the trained eye. A trained body language analyst can detect disharmony between your spoken words, main body signals, and micro signals. You just can't fake the micro signals. These are the involuntary signals that you give off unknowingly. For example, if someone tells you a lie with a smile on his face while holding his palms out, his micro body signals will give him away. His mouth may twitch, or the corners of his eyebrows may lift, which contradicts the message he's trying to pass across.

Chapter 2:   Why Analyze People?

We're inherently curious about why others think and feel the way they do. If a friend behaves unusually, we are quick to develop theories about the motivations and intentions behind their bizarre actions. Some people even pride themselves on being an excellent judge of character. Unluckily, we tend to rely merely on our past experiences and intuition when analyzing people, leading to inappropriate assumptions. There's a need to have a more precise way of interpreting the meaning behind the changes in a person's physiology. Learning the basics of analyzing what a person's body language says about their emotional state holds several benefits:

Control Social Situations

Humans are social beings, and there's no way around it. We instinctively crave for community and connection. Learning how to analyze others will enable you to understand them better on a deeper level. We are constantly broadcasting our identity through the way we present ourselves publicly. For instance, the clothes we wear can say a lot about how we would like others to view us. Underneath these superficial qualities, there's also sub-communicated information about our identity without our conscious awareness. For example, how we dress may express how insecure we are about ourselves because we're trying to cover up our personality's imperfections.

When you begin analyzing people, you'll notice that you start to uncover more interesting and more revealing information about others that's chiefly responsible for how they behave and feel.

Possessing the ability to observe and interpret social cues will also better equip you to handle all interactions with tact and diplomacy. As you incorporate these tips and techniques, your relationships, both professional and personal, will flourish as you deepen your understanding of the universal language of humans that is body language.

As of late, there's been an epidemic of self-proclaimed socially awkward people in the last decade. The current era of Facebook, text messaging, and Snapchat has shaped how an entire generation has developed socially. That's not to say that they have been stunted in their social development. Communicating through these new mediums is the quickest, most convenient way to express ourselves. However, when we communicate through these new mediums that solely rely on words, we lose the non-verbal aspects of communication. Also, unlike with non-verbal communication, we can easily lie with our words.

Even in this digital age of shopping for groceries on Amazon, some activities require us to have face-to-face interactions. In a world filled with people who are more accustomed to typing or texting behind a screen, learning how to analyze body language would give you a huge advantage in social situations. So, until absolutely everything can be accomplished from the comfort of your home without speaking to another human being, it's an excellent investment to work on your social intelligence.

Increase Emotional Intelligence

After learning how to read the body language of the people around you, you'll naturally begin to become more self-conscious.

It can be quite overwhelming to comprehend how the smallest of actions can expose how we feel at any given moment. This idea that people are equipped with the ability to read anyone's minds just by looking at them practically would make anyone feel extremely vulnerable.

The perfect course of action would be to take measures to control our body's physiology to convey to others how we want to be perceived. This requires us to be self-aware enough to know when we're sliding back into our default body language and then modifying it to portray ourselves the way we would like to be portrayed. You'll begin to recognize that our emotions can be influenced by how we position our bodies. The idea of deliberately placing ourselves in socially dominant stances to feel more self-confident has become a popular theory in the last decade.

Stances such as "The Wonder Woman," which require one to spread their feet a little wider than shoulder-width apart and place their hands on their hips, can make a person feel just as powerful and confident Amazonian heroine herself. When we modify the way we stand, we are proactive in managing our emotions. The truth is, so many of us allow our emotions to control our lives that we forget that we have emotions and that we are not our emotions.

By changing how we feel internally, it can transform our thoughts, beliefs, and behavior. To produce lasting changes, manipulating your body language as an emotional management technique requires diligence and practice, especially to turn this skill into a habit. At first, it'll take an overwhelming amount of effort to monitor our emotions since we haven't been conditioned to manage them. One way to accelerate this process is to integrate it into our social life to the point where it becomes our natural way of reacting to the world. It's easy to regulate your emotions when you're alone. It's much more challenging to practice this in the company of your friends and family.

Sometimes, our friends and family may say or do things that we don't agree with. It's not our responsibility to change these things about them, but we are always responsible for emotionally reacting to them. If you keep tabs on your feelings at any given moment and dissociate yourself from them in the toughest of scenarios, you'll make smarter decisions and take more deliberate action.

Spotting Deception

Everybody lies; the question is, how can we recognize when people lie before we suffer the consequences of their dishonesty? The ability to read people and figure out when they're lying is like a superpower that you can have. All it takes is to learn what to look out for in a person's body language and hone your observation skills, so you notice the signs every time they occur. The majority of the population is not aware that their dishonesty can be broadcasted publicly by their bodies. However skilled you may be at lying, it takes a lot of work for the brain to lie. We essentially need to hold on to two realities in our head, the reality of truth, and the reality we've conjured with our lies. It reaches a point where the brain is too preoccupied to ensure that the body's communication is in agreement with your lie, so it carelessly places your body on autopilot. Your body acts as an inadvertent tattletale when you lie while trying to ensure nobody knows that you're lying.

An illustration of this is when somebody is unable to maintain eye contact. When a person displays this behavior, there's a slight possibility that they are not telling the truth. This is the body's way of protecting itself from those who can potentially "punish" the individual if they're caught lying. If the eyes are the windows to the soul, constantly breaking eye contact suggests that your soul has something to hide. Sometimes, the body fails to suppress certain behavioral tics that indicate that what you're saying may not be in harmony with the truth. For example, if your coworker compliments the way you've dressed for work, but the facial muscles used for frowning slightly twitch, this may indicate that they are disingenuous with their compliment.

This sample brings up whether every lie is "sinister" and if you should expose every attempt at deceit you encounter. Would it be so terrible to go about your day believing that someone expressed a positive interest in the way you dress? Not at all! Some may prefer to live a life of blissful ignorance and wouldn't prefer to peek behind the curtain for fear that they'll regret learning the truth.

Chapter 3: Analyzing People via Their Verbal Statements

Our analysis and observation skills would be incomplete and inefficient if we ignore the significance of verbal statements. Verbal statements hold a myriad of keys into the doorways of our personalities, intentions, and emotions.

You can glean a lot from the words that you hear. Analyzing people through their verbal statements requires less effort and astuteness than that of nonverbal behaviors. We will take an in-depth look at how our words reveal our intentions, emotions, and personalities. I will include common speech clues you will come across in your daily interactions with those around you. Let's delve into this significant aspect of communication.

Understanding the Relationship between Words, Behavior, and Personality

Everything you do (nonverbal) or say (verbal) speaks volumes about your personality. When you become adept at analyzing people, you will realize that there's a synergy between our actions, thoughts, and beliefs and that each aligns to provide a full picture about who we are. Even though it seems insignificant compared to body languages, the words you use can tell a great deal about your desires, strengths, insecurities, and emotions.

How Words Reveal Your Personality

"Hey! Did you get taller overnight?" At first glance, this statement looks like a friendly banter, and it reveals no negative vibe. Now, if you look at the statement from another perception, you will realize that it allows us to glimpse the speaker's mind. In this context, the speaker cares a lot about the height difference. How did we know that?

If you think about snakes all day because you are scared of them, then you might easily confuse a skink for a snake.

In other words, we notice the things we care about. When you observe the friendly banter, you will realize that the person may be concerned about his height. This concern helped him to notice the height difference of his friend.

This statement could also stem from the speaker's insecurity about his height. Remember, when it comes to analyzing verbal statement, you need to consider the various factors at play, including watching the body language. In totality, both aspects of communication—verbal and nonverbal—are incomplete without the other.

Learn to Unclothe the Veil around Jokes

Two teenagers went to a restaurant. When the waiter came around to take their orders, one of the kids jokingly replied, "I want anything that costs a million dollars." To a casual observer, it is a normal and bland banter. To an astute observer, this kid is worried about money. Perhaps his family might be passing through some kind of financial crisis, or his parents and loved ones might have taught him the importance of money.

There's always a hidden message in every joke. Therefore, learning to analyze these jokes will give you a glimpse into the speaker's deepest desires and personality. You should know that the words people use have a deep meaning, irrespective of how well-crafted they are. A person might tell a joke to you without realizing he is revealing much more about his intentions. That is why it's easy to analyze those who make hurtful jokes to demean you.

Before we move to the next section, here's some advice: Never analyze a single phrase on its own. To not get incorrect results, try to observe the whole sentence, how the speech is conveyed, and the accompanying body language.

As a side note since we are talking about jokes, do you know the best sign that someone is intelligent? Humor. If you're looking to make connections with the smartest person in the room, find the one who makes others laugh the most.

Stories Are Powerful

It is easy to recognize a biased story, either verbally or in written form. You can effectively glimpse into the storyteller's psyche by listening to him or by reading his work. Here's an example for us to dissect:

From subject A's point of view: Last night, I was walking down a lonely street with my friends, and a large and muscular dark man appeared out of the neighboring bush and seemed to come toward us to attack. But he changed his mind in the last second and walked past us.

From subject B's point of view: Late in the evening, I took a stroll when I misplaced my keys in the nearby bush. It was already getting dark when I noticed I didn't have my keys on me. Time wasn't on my side since I needed to get home quickly to prepare for my date, so I searched and searched through the shrubs until I felt the keys. I jumped out onto the street in excitement and started running home. In my excitement, I nearly bumped into a group of frightened teenagers.

Both stories gave us different alert about the incident. The first point of view was from a teenager who didn't see the look of excitement on man's face. Rather, he emphasized the words huge, large, and dark. So why did he emphasize the physical attributes of the man who jumped out of the bush? Well, it's because that's the part that concerns him the most. He was scared because of the man's sudden appearance and physical size, which had a huge impact on the story. We have a full and clearer picture when you take a look at the other man's point of view, and that is the power of perception in stories.

So, when someone tells you a story, I want you to dissect the story and note the emphasized points of the story. By doing this, you will know how to analyze people effectively.

An Insight into How the Brain Process Words

There's something we have all come to agree on: the human brain is very efficient. We only use verbs and nouns when we think.

For instance, "I walked" or "I jumped." Adjectives, adverbs, and other speech parts are added during the latter phase of converting thoughts into written language or spoken words. The words that we add at this stage provide an insight into who we are and what we are thinking.

The basic and simple sentence consists of only a subject and a verb. For example, the verbal statement "I walked" consists of only the pronoun I (subject) and the verb's object. Any other word added to this basic sentence only modifies the verb's action or the quality of the noun. These deliberate additions or modifications provide insight into the writer or speaker's behavioral characteristics and personality.

Word clues help us to make behavioral guesses or develop hypotheses regarding the personality of others. Take a look at the verbal statement "I quickly walked." The word clue in this sentence is quickly since it serves as a modification of the verb walked. This word clue infused a sense of urgency in the statement, but it did not explain why. An individual can "quickly walk" because of the urgency of an appointment.

People who utilize this phrase are regarded as meticulous. Meticulous people are reliable and hate being late for an appointment since they respect societal norms and want to live up to expectations. These set of individuals will also make good employees since they don't want to disappoint their employees.

Conversely, you can also quickly walk when in a dark and lonely area with a bad reputation. Bad weather could also be the reason that you quickly walk.

In summary, people might make use of the word clue quickly walk for a variety of reasons. It's important to always read verbal statements about the circumstance surrounding the speaker or writer.

Word Clues You Need to Know

"I Labored Hard to Accomplish My Dreams"

The clue in this sentence is labored hard, and it shows that the person's dreams were difficult to accomplish. Perhaps it took him longer and harder to accomplish this particular dream than the other goals he has accomplished. When we delve deeper, you will discover that the word clue labored suggests the person holds the belief that dedication and hard work can produce great result.

"I Bagged Another Contract"

The word clue is another, and it reveals that the speaker or writer has won so many contracts and this is just the latest accomplishment. You can deduce that the speaker wants everyone who cared to listen to know that he won so many awards from the above sentence. He is trying to bolster his self-image by appearing successful. To an astute observer, this person seems self-conscious about what others think. More so, he needs the admiration of others to boost his self-esteem. Others who noticed this character weakness might try to exploit it for their gains.

"Jim and I Remained Friends"

The word clue in this sentence is remained. From the sentence, you can deduce that the speaker and Jim have gone through trying times. Perhaps the fabric of their friendship has gone through different difficult situations. They probably weren't supposed to be friends under normal circumstances. The speaker is trying to defend why she remained friend with Jim. The speaker doesn't feel convinced about her choice and, therefore, feels the need to defend her decision.

"I Patiently Sat Through the Meeting"

Here, the word clue patiently holds a plethora of hypotheses. For instance, the speaker might be bored with the lecture but felt obligated to sit through it for various reasons. Perhaps the speaker had to use the restroom but felt self-conscious or trapped from standing up to go the restroom. You could also deduce from the statement that she might have had an urgent appointment somewhere else.

Gauging from this statement, we can accurately say the speaker is someone who adheres to social etiquette and norms, irrespective of other pressing needs. Those with no social boundaries would have left the lecture to attend any other issue requiring their attention. People with social boundaries like the speaker would make good employees since they know how to follow the rules and respect authority.

Conversely, those who leave during the lecture to attend to other pressing needs are perfect candidates for jobs that require out-of-the-box thinking.

"I Decided to Buy That Dress"

The modifier or world clue here is decided. It indicates that the speaker weighed several options before settling for that particular dress. This statement shows us that the speaker is not impulsive. Rather, she weighs her options and takes the most logical step. More so, there's a high chance our speaker is an introvert since introverts tend to weigh their options before taking a step.

It's not a sure analysis, but a hypothesis about the speaker's personality. Conversely, an impulsive person would say, "I just bought that dress." The word clue just represents an impulsive decision.

Chapter 4:   How to Analyze Yourself

Through self-awareness, you gain an understanding of yourself and your personality. You can also get to know your behaviors and tendencies. Part of this process is coming to accept the unsightly corners of your mind that you would rather keep locked away. It is through embracing our whole being (even the darkness) that we can achieve true contentment. Some strategies listed below will allow you to take a closer look at the person you have become.

Be Aware of Your Feelings

Notice Your Thoughts

Your thoughts are essential in defining who you are. They will assist in guiding how you feel and your attitude and perceptions of situations. You should keep in touch with your mind. You need to be able to tell whether they are harmful if you are pinning yourself down, or within which areas you are hard on yourself? This reflection to encompass all of your perceptions, even the ones that need to change.

Keep a Journal

Keeping a journal can be a wonderful way to stay in tune with your patterns. Emotions and reactions will be documented. You can review the pages to gain an objective perspective on your values and consistency.

Be Conscious of Your Perceptions

Your perceptions can lead you astray, making you to come up with wrong conclusions about what occurred or what you saw. For instance, you can blame yourself that your friend was mad at you during lunch break; thus, you will think that you did something wrong. When you are conscious of your interpretation of her mood, this can assist you in knowing why you concluded that she is mad at you.

You are supposed to take your time to study your moves and beliefs about what happened with such situations. Write down what you saw, heard, or had feelings about that made you understand the situation the way you did. You must be able to get answers about what made your friend moody, and if there are any outside reasons, you should be aware of it.

Identify Your Feelings

The feelings you have will readily tell you the person you are, from how you react to situations you have at hand and the people around you. You are supposed to analyze your feelings and how you respond to different topics, interactions, tonal variations, facial appearances, and body language.

You should be able to tell why you have certain feelings and why you experienced such emotional responses. You should understand what you are responding to, and what directed you to make such choices. You are allowed to use physical cues to assist you in understanding how you feel.

Scrutinizing Your Values

Know Your Values

When you are aware of what you value, this can give you an overview of who you are at your core. Many of your beliefs are based on your individual experiences. They will change, the more you get to know about yourself. You may find it very difficult to identify your values at times. The concept can be intangible and unclear.

Identify Your Values

Values are the beliefs that you remain loyal to. They are usually based on morality. There are some things that you believe that others may not agree with. One of your core values may be to never steal. This is an idea you have thrown meaning behind, and you hold to this sentiment even when theft would benefit you in a significant way.

Your values describe the type of person you are. The caliber of friend or partner you are (to someone else) may be based upon these ideals, which you consider important. Defining unmoving moral mission statements can take some work! Imagine knowing off-hand, every aspect of yourself that you consider to be worthwhile. Most people aren't able to do this.

Start identifying your values by inscribing answers to questions like:

- Think two people you admire, what qualities do they have that make you admire them? What particular thing do they believe to make you admire them?

- Think of the person you hope to be in the future and write down all the positive aspects of their character.

- What are you passionate about?

- What good thing have you done, even when it would have been easier to walk away or take advantage?

Plan Your Core Values

When you have answered the above questions, you should have an idea of the qualities that you consider important. Writing these values down will allow you to create a map. Pick one or two of these at a time, and form a plan for being the sort of person who better embodies these beliefs. You have always been completely in control of the person you are. It can be so easy to forget that we are steering this vessel. Our daily grind can fog up the lens of our abilities. YOU decide all of the things that you wish to embody.

Do you look up to brave people? Right this moment, plan an activity that places you outside of your comfort zone. Do you want to be charitable? Call that homeless shelter, right this instant, and offer your services. You are being the steering wheel. You can be as cool, well-red, honest, or kind as you want to be.

Discover Yourself

Write Your Story

Writing down your story can be both fun and rewarding. This is your chance to document the events that changed you and the beliefs that you hold dear. Not only is this a brilliant way to pass the time, but it can also allow you to look back on your life, like a spectator. Can you imagine the feeling of accomplishment that will come from completing a project of this nature?

Evaluate Your Story

After writing down your story, you should be able to evaluate yourself by asking yourself questions like:

· What are some of the themes that recur in your narrative? Are you always saving people or you are the one who is always saved? Is your story based on a topic? Is it a love story, drama, comedy, or some other genre?

- What is the title of your story?

- What are the chapters your story is divided into?

- Have you labeled yourself and others in the story?

- What kind of words are you using to talk about yourself and the others? Are you using positive language?

Resolve What Your Analysis Means

You have to decide what your story means after writing it down. What is interesting about authoring your account, for review, will be referred to as narrative therapy. It will highlight your moments in life when you felt essential or worthy. It will also show you how you see yourself and the path of your life up to where you are.

For instance, you can tell your story as if it were a drama, due to a feeling that your life is dramatic and very intense. If it was written as a comedy, then you will think that your experience has been full of fun up to where you are. Or maybe it feels like a cosmic joke? A love story could indicate that you are a romantic.

Put it in Your Mind That it Takes Time

You can follow all the steps, but you still have to remember that it will need to take time. You should be aware that its vital to analyze yourself and put your ideas into action. The person you are will change in the days to come.

Track Your Sleeping

When you lack sleep, exhaustion will have some negative impacts on your body. This can encourage stress. You should be able to look at the hours you spend sleeping every night. Amount of sleep needed for an individual varies. This can result in your anxiety levels getting higher than they should be. When you don't sleep:

- You will think and learn slowly.

- There will be an increase in accidents.

- A lot of health challenges will be experienced.

- Increase in depression and forgetfulness.

- Lower libido.

- You will age faster.

- Weight will fluctuate.

- You will have impaired judgment.

You should have a list of things to help you to enhance your overall life experience. This will aid you in a thoughtful self-analysis. Brainstorm ways to promote growth. You should always see yourself evolving and changing based on your ambitions and life experiences.

It's extraordinarily vital to take your time and engage in self-analysis. This will assist you in changing into the person that you are meant to be. You can live by your values. You can make the rules and steer yourself toward realizing your goals.

Chapter 5:   Judging by the Cover

We've all been fed on the belief that judging a book by its cover is not the right way to do it. However, in a time and attention pressed world, where we rarely have the time to read people comprehensively, we seldom have an option but to analyze and speed people to make quick decisions. Reading a book by its cover or speed-reading people may not be such a bad thing today. People's outer appearances can often help you make solid and reliable conclusions about their personality. The subconscious visual that you form about an individual through their appearance is often accurate.

I know plenty of psychologists who believe that making snap judgments about people based on their appearances is an extremely narrow way of looking at it. However, the way a person treats themselves just as he/she treats his/her immediate environment can reveal a lot about their inherent personality. It can help you gain a deeper understanding of their personality to make communication even more meaningful.

The way a person dresses or maintains their outer appearance can reveal a lot about their internal feelings. Their exterior can often be a near accurate indicator of their thoughts, emotions, and feelings. Ever noticed how you don't bother about how your hair or face looks when you are completely dejected or sad. You don't have the inclination or zest to look good.

Similarly, when you feel more positive and upbeat, you will invest extra effort in looking good and feeling wonderful about yourself. People are well-dresses or sport a neatly-groomed appearance to gain respect or validation from others. They may want people to perceive them in a more positive light. It can also be a sign of high self-confidence, power, and authority. People in positions of power and authority may also be wealthy, which gives them the resources to be expensively dressed and groomed. It can be a sign of influence, power, and confidence. These folks are viewed in a more positive or flattering light by other people.

Here are some tips for reading people through their cover or outer appearance to make a near-accurate analysis of their personality or behavioral characteristics.

Good Influencers and Negotiators

Imagine a scenario where a plain-looking person is selling you something you don't need. He/she is plain looking and not very attractively dressed or groomed. Would you buy from him or her? The person doesn't appear like they are in a commanding or influential position when it comes to negotiations.

Now imagine another scenario where an extremely attractive, well-dressed, and nattily groomed salesperson walks up to you and introduces themselves to you. Again, you don't need what they are selling but you still listen to everything because they are cute-looking, friendly, and speak with oodles of charm. By the end of their sales pitch, you realize that you can use their product.

Attractive and well-groomed people have the power to influence people's decisions, however hollow it may seem. Of course, it isn't simply about wearing good clothes and looking good and ignoring everything else. There is a natural confidence and ease with which these people operate. Other factors such as friendliness, conversational skills, intelligence, and other things matter, too. This should explain why some people invest a bomb in maintaining their wardrobes and appearance.

Introverts and Extroverts

Extroverts thrive on adventure, new experiences, and risks. Their brains process dopamine starkly different than it is processed in a person who is more inward driven or introverted. These thrill-seekers think fast, act faster, and be more impulsive when it comes to decision making. They will move and walk fast, which means they are at a greater risk of injuries.

This can be slightly stretched to conclude that people who have more injury scars or casts have higher chances of being extroverts. Their thrill-seeking disposition and brain make them more prone to accidents and injuries. Yes, these people won't think twice before jumping out of a window to escape an adulterous confrontation.

Similarly, while introverts are more likely to observe your shoes and look at your feet while talking, extroverts will look you directly in the eyes while speaking. Since introverts are more inward driven and reflect upon their options before deciding, they tend to seize/observe people. There is a tendency to look down at a person's feet because of the awkwardness involved in looking away from a person while speaking rather than looking into their eyes. To avoid this uncomfortable situation of looking everywhere around the eyes, introverts will glance at a person's shoes or feet while thinking.

Since extroverts are more outward driven and focused, they will look people in the eyes while talking. There is a tendency to experience rather than think, which means all their efforts are directed towards experiencing or listening to people instead of thinking about what people are talking about. They'll seldom look in different directions (unless they are lying or there's another clear reason for the mismatch in behavior) and will have their eyes firmly fixated on their speaking.

Blue eyes and light, blonde hair has almost always been closely linked with introversion. However, there isn't a conclusive study to support this view. More than anything, it is a popularly peddled media notion that is completely supported by the Hollywood and Disney brigade.

There is a definite bias towards light eyes and hair each time a character has to be represented as an introvert. Ariel, Belle, and Hercules are all Disney characters who've been portrayed as introverts with light hair and eyes. Today, you can't go about judging people's personalities through the color of their eyes or hair because people are dying their hair and changing colored contact lenses faster than you can say personality.

Reading People through Their Clothes

How a person dresses reveals a lot about their personality. Neatly dressed and groomed people may have an inherent need to be respected and accepted within their social group. They may have a deep need to fit in or be validated by others. At times, dressing excessively well or paying too much attention to one's appearance can sign narcissism or self-obsession. The person may also be suffering from a deeply-rooted inferiority complex or low self-esteem that they are trying to compensate for by dressing well.

Sometimes, people who pay too much attention to their grooming and appearance may believe that they aren't good enough for anything and may use their looks to cover up for the perceived inadequacies in their life.

One of my friends could never match up to her older sibling when it came to intelligence, social skills, and talent. While the parents lavishly praised her older sister for being an intelligent and talented student, she (the younger sibling) wasn't believed to be striking or extraordinary in anything. She believed she wasn't good at anything throughout her growing up years and sought constant validation from people through her looks and clothes. She became obsessed with her appearance and spent huge sums of money on grooming, beauty products, beauty treatments, and makeovers.

Thus, an excessive need to look good and dress well can also be a clue to an inferiority complex marked personality. Know more about a person before you make snap judgments about their outer appearance. However, appearance and other nonverbal clues can offer you plenty of insights about an individual's subconscious thoughts, feelings, and preferences.

Chapter 6: Is Someone Uncomfortable Around Me?

One thing that we need to take a look at when we are analyzing someone is how comfortable they are with us. If they are comfortable, their stance is going to be more relaxed. They will offer us more information about themselves; have more open expressions, and so much more.

But when someone is feeling uncomfortable with you, this will spell out some trouble for you as well. This is going to make it harder for you to talk with them. They may even inch away from you in the hopes of ending the conversation before you have a chance to get to know them.

So, one of the first things you need to explore is whether someone is comfortable or uncomfortable around you. As soon as you notice that someone is uncomfortable with the situation or with you in particular, you can start to take the proper steps to get them at ease and feeling better.

Now, how do you make sure that you can meet up with someone and ensure that they are as comfortable with you as possible? Some of the signs that you should watch out to tell if someone is uncomfortable with you or in that situation will include the following:

The Flinch or Wince

When we find ourselves in an awkward situation, it is never fun, and it is going to cause people to wince literally. When someone feels uncomfortable, but they don't want to let others know, they may wince or flinch a bit. This is going to be a quick contraction of the torso away from you. And the wince is going to be like they stubbed their toe, or got a paper cut. They often don't realize they are doing it or don't want you to know about it because they are polite. But, if you do pick up on this with the other person, take note of what is causing that reaction.

They Back Away from You

When someone feels uncomfortable, they may take a step back from you without realizing what they are doing. If they aren't able to move away from you or the situation, they will see how much they can close themselves. This can include turning away, crossing the arms and legs, and retreating in the torso.

This process is known as blocking body language. This is something we can do without thinking about it as a way to protect ourselves. Suppose you are with another person and notice that they are doing these actions. In that case, it may be a good idea to respect their personal space (remember that each person has a different idea of what their own space is and how large it is), consider taking a step back, and allow them the space they need to get comfortable.

Their Words and Gestures Get Faster

Any time you are around another person who does not feel that comfortable, they may have a sense of fight or flight. And in this situation, they are going to start moving their arms wildly. And in some cases, they are going to start talking faster. This is because the person feels that their breath and the beat of their heart goes faster. When this happens, it will include their speech and gestures accelerating because it allows them to get the conversation done with.

Their Laughter Is Nervous

Nervous laughter is another thing that we need to take a look for when trying to figure out how comfortable someone is around us. We have all heard the difference between real laughter and nervous laughter. This nervous laughter is often going to erupt, and it is a way for us to release some of the tension found inside. This is why they may giggle or laugh at things that would seem odd to another person.

The Tone of Their Voice Changes

One of the first things that we will notice when we are talking to someone nervous around us is the tone of their voice. We can notice this if we know the person from before, and we know what the usual tone of their voice is, but we can also see this with someone we have never talked to in the past.

When someone is nervous, it is sometimes going to appear in a loud and squeaky voice. This is because we have an increased amount of stress because of that situation. The voice is often going to rise in pitch, and it will sound shriller than before. As the stress rises in the individual, the tension will rise, causing some issues with the vocal cords.

They Have Trouble Maintaining Their Eye Contact

If someone is comfortable with you and doesn't mind spending some time talking with you, they will have no problem talking to you and maintaining good eye contact. But when someone keeps looking at their watch, glancing over their shoulder, or seeming like they can look everywhere besides at you, this is a good sign that they are not enjoying the conversation.

This one often needs a few more signs to go along with it. It could mean that they are not interested in the conversation. It could mean that you are dominating the situation and the conversation, or it could mean that there is something with you or the conversation or the situation around you that makes the person feel uncomfortable.

When this does happen, it is an excellent time to pause and take a break from the conversation. You can stop talking and then ask the other person what they think or what views they hold on the subject. Then, give them some time to talk to you without interrupting. The answer that they provide will help you know if this is a conversation that the person is interested in continuing or something you need to stop and move on with.

The Answers They Give Are Only One or Two Words Long

If someone is comfortable with you and is enjoying the conversation, then their words are just going to flow out of them. This is true even if you and the other person have just met each other. But, if you get into a conversation with someone and you find that they are only giving one-word answers, then this is a sign that they aren't interested in the conversation, that they are distracted, or that they are shy and don't know how to make the conversation go more.

This may take a bit more work to get the person to open up and talk with you a bit more. If the person is shy, you need to change your tactics to get them to be more comfortable and open up a little more. For example, make sure that you show interest in them, and see if it helps only ask questions that need a more detailed answer, rather than ones that can be answered with yes or no.

Their Ears Get Red, Or They Scratch Their Nose

These are signs that someone is not that comfortable in the situation, but they are more subtle signs that are easy to miss out on or assume are not that important at all. When these shows up though, you know for sure that the other person is not feeling at ease in the situation and that you need to approach them differently.

If you are talking to someone who seems to blush when they feel embarrassed or nervous, you already have a good idea that having a red face is a big sign of someone not being comfortable with the situation. But some people are going to blush in a less obvious manner. This means that you need to watch out for places other than the face that starts to red. You want to watch the ears in particular because this is an early sign that the other person feels out of place.

In addition to watching the color of the ears of the other person you are talking to, it is also a good idea to watch the other person and how often they are scratching their nose. If they only do this once in the whole conversation, then this is not a big deal. But if you see them doing this all of the time, then this is a good sign that they are feeling nervous, and that you may need to lighten up the conversation and help them feel more at ease.

One thing that a lot of people don't realize is that an increased amount of blood flow to the face is going to cause the nose to feel itchy. The nose is going to have a ton of blood vessels in it. And when we are under stress, which can happen when we feel nervous or like we don't belong, the flow of the blood can increase, and a lot of that will end up in the blood vessels of the nose. This causes it to itch and can be a sign that there is some uneasiness going on.

As you can see from this, along with some of the other topics that we will explore in this guide, body language will do a lot to tell us what the other person thinks and how they are feeling. It even helps us to know if someone is feeling a bit uncomfortable around us or not.

If you find that you are the one who is the source, although sometimes, it could be another person, the situation, or something else, then you may find that giving someone a bit of space and offering up a quick apology for it can help them to relax. Saying something like, "I'm sorry if I'm a bit much. I get onto a topic and get so excited that I overdo it. I would love to hear your opinion on XYZ!" This helps to let the other person know that you are not trying to make them feel uncomfortable, and can get things back on track for you.

Chapter 7:   Lies

Do you know that you are lied to more than ten times a day by the people who are close to you? When people lie, they make something that is not true and seem to be the naked truth.

Everyone looks at lying as a bad habit, but this does not stop them from lying. The lies start when we are still kids, and it goes on into adulthood. The sad thing is that when lying goes beyond the boundaries, it becomes a destructive habit to many people. Let us start by looking at the different types of lies.

Types of Lies

White Lie

White lies are more of an excuse not to do something and are told with the intention of font spoiling your relationship.

However, telling white lie after white lie will lead to conflict later when the person realizes that you have been lying to them. You will end up losing credibility in front of the family and friends.

Broken Promise

When you promise someone something, you need to go ahead and fulfill it. Broken promises refer to a commitment that you fail to a jeep. If you did not have the intention to fulfill the promise, you end up making things worse.

Fabrication

Fabricating something is telling someone something, which you do not know for sure if it is true. You just come up with something then you say it. When you spread a rumor, you will be like stealing another person's reputation.

Bold-faced Lie

This is a lie that you tell, and everyone knows that it is a lie. The signs will be there that you tell a lie, but since you know, it is a bold one; you just say it while maintaining a straight face.

Now that you know what types of lies are there, the next thing you need to know is why people lie in the first place.

Why Do People Lie?

Fear

People lie because they are afraid of the consequences of the truth. They will tell a lie because they know that they have done something that you do not like. So, they try to cover up the crime so that you do not get to know what they did.

Manipulation

A person will tell you lie so that they can manipulate the truth. The lie is motivated by the desire to get someone to say something or to do it, or to make a decision that will favor the liar in one way or another. Many people lie to get something, such as money, sex, status, or power.

Pride

In many instances, the person will lie because they are too proud. They use the line as a way to display a favorable image. They will exaggerate so much that you will not know what is true.

Why Is Lying such a Big Deal?

Why is it that we focus on lying so much? The truth is that when you lie, you change so many aspects of yourself for someone else. Let us look at the disadvantages of lying.

Lying Can Affect Your Health

People that lie have to keep the guilt for a very long time. They will keep unpleasant secrets that can even lead to health complications.

You Will Live a Stressful Life

People that lie get to release stress hormones.

It Makes You Lonely

When you lie, people tend to alienate you because they cannot trust you. You will face the punishment that people will not believe you, and you will not believe anyone. When people alienate you, you end up having no one to share with.

It Becomes a Habit

When you lie, you will make it a routine such that even the things that do not need you to lie end up being lines in themselves.

You Have to Remember a Lot

When you lie, you have to think of what you said about the lie, how you said it, and how you said it. If you have many lies, you will find it a huge bid on you, and it might cause a lot of unnecessary stress. By the time, you start remembering what you said and how you said it, you will be open showing that it was a blatant lie.

You Become Unreliable

When you lie, people will take you the way you present yourself – as a liar. Even your partner and other people close to you will not believe in you and will not trust you at all.

Chapter 8:   Speed Reading

Speed reading is one of the most popular and powerful methods used to identify differences in people. It is used to gain an in-depth understanding of people types and how this affects their behavior.

Speed reading utilizes several proven techniques to help you understand other people's motivations and emotions so that you can customize your approach to them for a more effective impact. In simple terms, speed-reading refers to the ability to read other people quickly and using this to influence their decisions and abilities. Speed-reading involves reading a person's body language signals. The difference between this and other types of people reading is that speed-reading does not involve the study of hundreds of nonverbal signals. Instead, the reader uses some form of intuition to gain information about others.

To be effective in speed-reading, it is advised that you focus on big signals, not the small ones. This technique involves concentrating on the other person and knowing when to trigger a conversation with them. These conversations will sometimes go well but flop at other times. As you converse with people, you must be quick enough to grasp some of your mind's evident signals to process.

The essence of speed-reading is to eliminate the struggle people go through to capture every signal sent by others. When you spend a lot of time trying to process these signals, the conversation may end as soon as it begins. It is not easy to be talking to someone while your mind is busy processing every kind of movement that the person makes. Doing this eliminates the possibility of identifying exactly what the person is thinking or feeling. To keep it simple, try applying the technique of speed-reading. Focus on the big movements and ignore the small ones.

For instance, a person who is bored with the conversation will always withdraw eye contact or turn to face the opposite direction. Smiling or nodding of the head automatically shows you that the person is happy. When it comes to speed reading, you should not waste your time trying to unlock the meaning of things you do not understand. When you do this, you may end up with the wrong interpretation of the person, resulting in the wrong judgment.

Speed Reading and the Law of Reverse Effect

Speed-reading is something that is done by the subconscious mind. Forcing your conscious mind to perform this duty results in what is known as the law of reverse effect. When looking for information to read from the other person, you may once in a while overthink some signals and start processing them beyond the subconscious mind. This can make you appear too distant from the conversation. The best way to avoid this is by allowing your unconscious mind to do all the processing. Trust your intuitions and gut instincts. This will help you to understand some signals without having to think deeply about their meaning.

Instincts are derived from real science. It is believed that some of the hollow organs of the body, like intestines, contain nerves that act as a secondary brain that transmits signals to the main brain. This is why a person's intuition is often referred to as his 'gut instincts.' Intuition is a way of the mind indicating that it already has received some information about the situation at hand.

Another most important aspect of speed-reading is the ability to remain calm during times of discomfort. This is one of the easiest ways that boost your ability to speed read other people. When you are at peace, it is easier to relax during weird circumstances, and this means that you will be able to handle any tension that arises when things get tough. One way to achieve this is through mindful breathing. You can do this by concentrating on certain simple exercises that help you slowly breathe in via your nose and breathe out through the mouth. This helps you to relax your panic muscles as you continue to read others.

Speed Reading and Receptiveness

Some people often try as much as possible not to send any non-verbal signals to others. Most salespeople and those whose roles involve negotiation often do this. You can get these people to reveal their true thoughts and feeling by doing something they least expect from you. This will cause them to be distracted, and as a result, they will display some genuine reactions. For instance, you can tease them in a friendly manner, or ask rhetorical questions that will stir their emotions at once.

You may also decide to use what is known as provocative therapy. This involves an act of trying to convince them otherwise or by bluffing them. This will confuse the person who will then reveal his true identity. Practicing these strategies while remaining focused can help you grow faster to become an expert in speed-reading.

Several guidelines apply when it comes to speed-reading; these are:

- Adopting the best approach – just like we said earlier, do not get distracted trying to read every signal sent your way. Also, you should avoid thinking ahead of what is happening at the moment. The process of speed-reading involves specifying exactly what you want to know from a person and concentrating on it.
- Monitor your Eye Movement – control the way you move your eyes. This is because the other person may also be skilled in seed reading and therefore, they might get the wrong signal just by observing your eye movement
- Maintain a certain pattern – speed-reading needs a sense of pattern or rhythm. Assess the person one trait or signal at a time. You may make a pre-list of the things you wish to find out and use this list to analyze the person. Avoid revisiting old signals and concentrate on learning something new, unless if it is necessary
- Process ideas, not words – when interacting with others, do not focus more on the words but the words' signals. The faster you read someone, the better for you since some people tend to hide their real emotions as the conversation continues. Seek knowledge about some of the signals that other people send. This will speed up the process of visualizing meaning from other people's reactions. As a result, reading sessions will be made shorter and more effective.
- Suppress your bad habits – human behavior is made of a collection of habits. It is ideal that when speed reading,

you identify some of the bad habits you have and slowly work on minimizing them.

Speed-reading other people have a good number of benefits. One of them is that the technique trains your mind to become more focused, thus improving its processing capacity and capability. It also gives you a better understanding of others, and this influences how you treat them in the future. Speed-reading always flexes the brain and exercises brain muscles. This translates to better memory retention, and as a result, you will be able to become more alert during speed-reading sessions.

As you speed-read others, you may identify some information and traits that will improve your personality. Once you master the art of speed-reading, you will always appear more confident when with your peers, who will also see you as an emotionally intelligent person. You may also identify several new opportunities as you speed-read people. This is because most of them will trust your abilities and may recommend some good opportunities. Your ability to grasp things quickly will always act as a plus, and you will easily assimilate data, which you can use to innovate new strategies and ideas. Once you master the art of speed-reading, your confidence may pave the way for leadership positions, and this will result in better earnings in terms of salaries and allowances.

In conclusion, learning how to speed read requires a lot of patience. You must be a person that grasps processes and information easily. Even without a real speed reading session, you must be able to practice this technique frequently to become better at it.

Chapter 9: Cold Reading

Cold reading is known to be a con artist's best friend. It provides the illusion of mind reading and magical abilities without the use of actual supernatural power. It is often used by those who make a living through fortune-telling and psychic acts. Many people have been completely sold on the act. It is usually performed by someone who excels in reading others, has acquired enough general knowledge, and has practiced enough to deliver a very believable performance. However, such an act is only a form of psychology, and you could create this act yourself if you choose to. You would do this by creating the illusion of knowing more than you do through the power of observation. There are different names for the different techniques. How many people are present decides how you should approach it. Shot gunning, for instance, is done in a large room packed with people. This is often the choice of mediums who are creating the illusion of connecting to a passed loved one, because whatever they say, there is likely to be someone who can relate to the statement. When the medium speaks a few, usually vague, phrases, such as "I am connecting to an elderly man... the name John or Jack comes to mind. Does that speak to anyone?" he or she watches for anyone who expresses recognition. Jack and John's names are very common, and many people have lost a grandfather in their time. The medium will then choose one person and watch their face carefully. This is where the true psychology steps in.

Reading body language is essential to keeping up the ruse, as the medium will need to narrow down the descriptions of the audience members loved one. If, for example, the medium says something about a white picket fence, yet no familiarity comes to this person's face, he or she will have to carefully change their tactic. He or she might explain that he never lived within a white picket fence, but wanted to, or that another relative was also present. If the audience member agrees or seems excited, this medium will know they are getting warmer. This act is continued, and even peppered by what are known as rainbow ruses. These are contradictory phrases such as "He was a gentle man; however, he would occasionally display a stern side". Most people have experienced these contradictory moments in their personality; however, the word choice feels so specific that it seems as if it only applies to the supposed spirit the man or woman is referring to.

Another cold reading method, which may be more suitable to a smaller population, is to use previous knowledge when observing someone's behavior. This method is often used in detective dramas, as the act is dramatic and exciting to watch, and the character appears intelligent and clever. It is, however, easier than it may appear, as it only takes keen observation skills. For example, if you meet a new person and notice there is graphite smudged along the side of their left hand, you will know that they are left-handed, as those who are left-hand dominant must drag their hand along the previously written words to continue writing. As a left-hander myself, I would know. This phenomenon, which has been jokingly called "The Silver Surfer Syndrome", is an unquestionable indication that this person is left-handed. You may say so with confidence as you shake their hand. The confident statement will shock this person, and they won't think to look for physical indicators. This can be used as a fun trick to amuse others, or as a shocking factor to carry into a persuasive technique, as those who have recently been surprised don't always think every factor of a decision through.

Cold reading, as any other manipulation tactic, can be used on anyone. And it is. Many people studied in the ways of cold reading have used it as a career, such as psychics, fortune-tellers, and any kind of con artist. Such a complicated set-up is unnecessary to add this skill to your toolbox, as you only need your observation and shock factor. Another example is if you see someone you may already know is a student, you could confidently exclaim that they were studying late and fell asleep on their work as you note the imprint of math work on their left ear. These subtle observations build up over time, and you may gain a reputation with that person. The more you get to know someone, the more background information you will have stored away. For example, say you have a friend named Kyle. Kyle is a single father of an adorable six-year-old girl he spends every moment he can with. To support her, he works at a grueling desk job where he files paperwork all day long and takes rude phone calls. You know that he likes light coffee with a lot of sweetener, and that he is right-handed.

Today, Kyle arrives with a large coffee in his left hand. You two always meet up every Tuesday around ten in the morning. Today, it's almost eleven. In the back of his car is a pink hairbrush. When he gets close enough to greet you, you smell the strong aroma of black coffee rising from his cup, and you can see his clothes are wrinkled. Without asking him, what can you deduce from his situation?

I believe that his boss kept him very late and piled on the work the night prior. He's gotten papercuts before; however, even the light touch of his coffee seems too much pain this time, so he was working as quickly as possible. Even so, he got home late that night and overslept the next morning. Rushing to get her to school, Kyle likely tossed his daughter's hairbrush back to do her best with her hair on their way to school. Due to his exhaustion, he stopped to buy a coffee much stronger than he likes it before meeting with you. What situations you come to find yourselves observing will vary, as will the indicators that you notice.

You can also use cold reading to gather information you don't have, by acting as if you do. For example, if you are a business salesman in a clothing shop who encounters a shy, young girl that is close to the age of high school, you may focus on this observation to begin with. You could state or ask with confidence if she has an event coming up. It doesn't hurt to be aware of large school events nearby, as there may be a dance she wants to prepare for. She may nod or shrug. Either response isn't a no. After, you could press on and ask if she wants to wear something that will catch a certain someone's attention. Because she's shy, she may have difficulty speaking about her feelings to that cute boy from her math class. Or, she may even want to look nice to feel superior to that girl who bullies her about her looks. Either way, this vague statement will technically be correct. With this much information, you can gather that she'll want to look elegant. Taking a look at her clothes that she currently has on will give you a clue as to her preference with style. If she's wearing long sleeves and baggy pants, she won't feel inclined to reveal something. You can work with this in two ways. You could persuade her to buy the dress with a low back and no sleeves by explaining how confident she'll appear while that yellow brings out the color in her eyes, or you could take the safer approach and find her a nice dress with long sleeves and a high neckline. This whole time, the girl never told you what she wanted or why she needed a dress, but you learned enough to make the sale anyway.

Cold reading isn't only useful in sales clerk settings and parlor tricks. You can also use it to gain a favor, shock someone into doing as you wish, and learning enough about another person to use to your advantage.

Chapter 10: How to Spot Insecurity

When someone is behaving irrationally, you have to remind yourself that this could be because they are acting out of a certain emotion. It could also be because their insecurity is behind this false sense of bravado. When you notice this, you will more likely procure a sense of empathy for these people who act arrogantly or rudely because what they are trying to do is covering their insecurity.

Their insecurity can be about anything—looks, power, money, smartness, getting better grades, and so on—and most of these insecurities creep out from a sense of material value. Sometimes, insecurity can be justified—but most of the time, it is not. Insecurity manifests differently, and it can range from the inability to accept that they've done a great job or accept a compliment to as far as not wanting to wear a swimsuit to the beach.

Factors Determining Good and Bad

None of these traits helps us to behave virtuously. There is a fine line between being insecure and being a brat. Here are some identifying factors that can help you separate the good and the bad:

1. Self-kindness is not self-judgment.

Compassion towards someone insecure is understanding and being warm to them when they fail, when they suffer or when they feel inadequate. We should not be ignoring these emotions or criticizing. People who have compassion understand that being human comes with imperfections and failing is part of the human experience. There will inevitably be no failure when we attempt something because failure is part of learning and progress. Having compassion is also being kind with yourself when challenged with painful experiences rather than getting angry at everything and anything that falls short of your goals and ideals.

Things cannot be exactly how it should be or supposed to be or how we dream it to be. There will be changes and when we accept this with kindness and sympathy and understanding, we experience greater emotional equanimity.

2. Common humanity and not isolation

It is a common human emotion to feel frustrated especially when things do not go the way we envision them to be. When this happens, frustration is usually accompanied by irrational isolation, making us feel that we are the only person on earth going through this or making dumb mistakes like this. News flash—all humans suffer, all of us go through different kinds of suffering. Compassion involves recognizing that we all suffer and all of us have personal inadequacies. It does not happen to 'me' or 'I' alone.

3. Mindfulness is not over-identification.

Compassion needs us to be balanced with our approach so that our negative emotions are neither exaggerated nor suppressed. This balancing act comes out from the process of relating our personal experiences with that of the suffering of others. This puts the situation we are going through into a larger perspective.

We need to keep mindful awareness to observe our negative thoughts and emotions with clarity and openness. Having a mindful approach is non-judgmental and it is a state of mindful reception that enables us to observe our feelings and thoughts without denying them or suppressing them. There is no way that we can ignore our pain and feel compassion at the same time. By having mindfulness, we also prevent over-identification of our thoughts and feelings.

Discovering Compassion

You're so dumb! You don't belong here loser! Those jeans make you look like a fat cow! You can't sit with us! It's safe to say we've all heard some kind rude, unwanted comments either directly or indirectly aimed at us. Would you talk like this to a friend? Again, the answer is a big no.

Believe it or not, it is a lot easier and natural for us to be kind and nice to people than to be mean and rude to them whether it is a stranger or someone we care about. When someone we care is hurt or is going through a rough time, we console them and say it is ok to fail. We support them when they feel bad about themselves and we comfort them to make them feel better or just to give a shoulder to cry on.

We are all good at being understanding and compassionate and kind to others. How often do we offer this same kindness and compassion to ourselves? Research on self-compassion shows that those who are compassionate are less likely to be anxious, depressed or stressed and more resilient, happy and optimistic. In other words, they have better mental health.

Identifying Someone with Insecurity

When we can identify when a person is acting out of insecurity can enable us to protect ourselves from engaging in a mindless power play and feel insecure ourselves. Insecure people tend to spread their negativity and self-doubt to others as well and here is how you can identify them and decide whether to show compassion or show them the exit:

#1 people who are insecure try to make you feel insecure yourself.

You start questioning your ability and self-worth and this happens when you are around a specific person. This individual can manipulate you and talk about their strengths and how they are good in this and that and in a way try to put you down. They project their insecurities on you.

#2 insecure people need to showcase his or her accomplishments.

Inferiority is at the very core of their behavior and for people like this, compassion to tell them that they are not what they think in their heads is just a waste of your time. They feel insecure and hide it, talk about their accomplishments, not in a good way but constantly brag about their amazing lifestyle, wonderful shoes, huge cars, and elite education. All of this is done to convince themselves that they do have it all and you have none.

#3 people who are insecure drops the "humble brag" far too much.

The humblebrag is essentially a brag that is disguised as a self-derogatory statement. In this social media age, you can see plenty of humblebrags who complain about their first-world problems such as all the travel they need to do or the amount of time they spend watching their kids play and win games or even the person who complains about having a tiny pimple when the rest of their face looks flawless. Social media is ripe with people who are narcissistic and this is not worth your time. Do not feel any less just because someone shows off how much of traveling, they need to do.

#4 people who are insecure frequently complain that things aren't good enough.

They like showing off the high standards that they have and while you may label them as snobs, it might be a harder feeling to shake off because you might be thinking that they are better than you although you know that it is all an act. They proclaim their high standards to assert that they are doing better than everyone else and make you feel less of yourself and miserable. Pay no attention to people like this.

It does make sense that people who have better self-esteem and compassion as if you are happier and optimistic about your future without having to worry about what insecure people have to say. When we continuously criticize ourselves and berate ourselves because we think other people are winning at life, we feel incompetent, worthless, and insecure ourselves, which these people want us to feel. This negativity cycle is vicious and will continue to self-sabotage us, and sometimes, we end up self-harming ourselves.

But when our positive inner voice triumphs and plays the supportive friend's role, we create a sense of safety and accept ourselves enough to see a better and clear vision. We then work towards making the required changes for us to be healthier and happier. But if we do not do this, we are working ourselves towards a downward spiral or chaos, unhappiness, and stress.

Chapter 11: How to Spot Romantic Interest?

If we had the definite guide to spot a romantic interest, Tinder would go broke. That said, it is not hard to identify the telltale signs if someone is interested in you. Granted that some people are oblivious to it—but if you do focus, you'd come to the realization if that person is indeed romantically interested in you or if they are just being flirtatious.

Usually, that special someone starts with a casual acquaintance, which leads to friendship—and before you know it, you look at this friend in a different light and keep thinking about them. Do they feel the same way you feel? Identifying if someone is interested in you romantically requires the careful and skillful interpretation of signals and actions.

Ways to Figure Out If Someone Is Romantically Interested

Here are 15 ways to figure out if someone is romantically interested in you or if they are just flirting for the thrill of it

#1 Their conversations with you

Conversations, meaningful ones are ways a person shows a deeper interest in you and what you do. Do they keep asking you questions in an attempt to keep the conversation going? Pay attention to the questions they ask because it can tell you if they are genuinely showing interest in the things you do and like. A good and long conversation about your likes, dislikes, favorite music and so on is a classic sign of someone genuinely liking you and your company. If you are enjoying the conversation and the other person is engaging in it without looking bored or yawning, this is a sign that both parties are equally interested in each other.

#2 They keep bumping into you.

Call it fate but this can also be a sign that they like you and engineering any possible opportunities to meet you. This is sweet but also can be creepy if it becomes too much like stalking. If you feel that this person is following you or you suddenly feel uncomfortable, listen to your gut feeling and make a report. Stalking is serious and dangerous. If the person keeps bumping into you happens to be at places like the cafeteria or the lunchroom or neighborhood coffee place and not specific places like your gym that you've been going to for years, your house or anyway specific and private – make a complaint.

#3 They discuss plans.

Another sign that someone could be romantically interested in you is to plan for more dates or start talking about the near future because they see you in it. It isn't about plans to get married or buy a house but merely simple things like a concert in your area that they'd like to take you or even a friend's party in a week that they'd like you to come with. They have these upcoming events and they'd like you to be part of it.

#4 Five more minutes

If someone is interested in you, chances are they would like to spend a few more minutes longer with you. They don't mind adjusting their schedule just so they can spend an extra 5 more minutes to talk to you or even spend that extra 5 minutes on the phone just so they can continue talking to you. The fact that they do this is also an indication that they have romantic feelings for you.

#5 Reasons to spend time together

'I'm in the area—want to grab a bite?' or 'Oh you're having a cold? I can make a mean chicken soup—I'll bring it over' or even 'What are you doing right now? Want to go have dinner together?' Make no mistake that these could just be that the person likes spending time with you simply because you are a cool person to hang out with but if these reasons keep piling up and it only involves just the two of you, it is probably a big sign that this person likes you.

#6 Observe their body language.

If someone likes you, they mirror your body language and your movements. They sit in closer, they lean in, they smile when you smile, they find ways to touch you (not in a creepy way) like brushing against your shoulder, putting a strand of your hair behind your ear – all these are classic flirtation signs and if you are uncomfortable, say so. Still, if you are enjoying it, this person is clearly into you.

#7 The compliments are mountainous.

Complimenting someone excessively can be a sign of ass-kissing or just trying to be nice. But if this person compliments you sincerely, it could be that they are interested in you. Look out for verbal cues such as complimenting your fashion choice or the way you style your hair. It could be that they are just being friendly, but them dropping compliments every time you meet is a big sign of them being interested in you.

#8 They remember the little things.

The closer you get to know someone—the more information you divulge to them. Your romantic interest will pick up many interesting things about you and save it in their long-term memory. These things can be your favorite color, your favorite ice cream flavor, the first movie you watched together, where you first met – all of this is an indication that this person is genuinely interested in you.

#9 Conversation starters

Some people are shy and are not big talkers so while this is something to take note of, you cannot be the only one initiating contact all the time. If someone is willing to connect despite being shy, that means they want to talk to you. Having one-way initiations for everything is a definite NO that the other person doesn't like you and do not see the need to spend the time to talk or even meet you but if they initiate contact as much as you do, that is a sure sign that they are into you.

#10 Other people are off-limits.

Take note of when a person talks about someone else—do they talk a lot about other girls or guys when they are with you? Or is the conversation focused on just you and your person? What a person says in a conversation and how they refer to other people in their social circle can give you real clues into whether they are romantically interested in you. Talking about going on a date with a girl or guy is not a good indication that this person likes you.

Trusting your feelings and your intuitions in all these possible scenarios above is the best bet. Remember that different people do different things to show someone they care or are interested in them and cultural values, upbringing, and societal norms also play a big part in identifying these signs so nothing is set in stone. All the signs described above are a good telling sign that a person is interested in you especially if they like spending more time with you. Even if you are not sure, you can exhibit signs that you are interested in them so that they will also have an idea but to be on the safest side, telling someone that you like them. You'd like to get to know them better and even start dating is the best way forward to prevent any miscommunication or misunderstanding between two people.

Of course, the game of love is not as straightforward and as simple as it is. It takes a little bit of dating experience to figure out if someone is into you or not or you can just do the good old fashion trial and error, get your heart broken, kiss all the toads till you meet your prince or princess charming.

Chapter 12:   How to Spot Dangerous Person?

There are always people at the extremes of each trait and, sometimes, these people can be dangerous. While most people exhibit a fair few 'good' personality traits, and perhaps a couple of 'bad' ones, some people exhibit a singular bad trait so strongly or even several bad traits at a low level. Such people can be anything from mildly annoying, lacking in social skills, downright manipulative or abusive. Most concerning is the fact that some people can mask these negative traits quite well. How many times have you met someone you thought was friendly enough to realize later that they are not someone you want to know at all? What about friends you have who act one way in one situation but can be completely different at other times? Everyone would do well to remember that no matter how good we get at analyzing and speed-reading others, there is always a chance that something important will escape our notice, or that the other person will be able to mask their intentions too well.

Despite this, there are some red flags for which we can learn to look out. These apply to all of our relationships – not just romantic ones. Identifying personality types that may harm us involves understanding what healthy relationships look like, whether they are with family members, friends, colleagues, superiors, and yes, romantic or sexual partners. Here is a list of some telltale signs that something's wrong in your interaction with another person. Their behavior points to their personality – and if their personality is harming you, you are always within your rights to step back, get out, and look for support to ensure your safety, physically, emotionally, and mentally. Identifying

64

one of these red flags in your relationship with someone doesn't mean you have to cut ties with them immediately, but it should give you pause about how you'd like things to change in the future.

Red Flags

- Give and take: All relationships should be two-sided; there has to be give and take on both sides. Of course, the give and take will naturally wax and wane in all relationships, and in some cases, an uneven weighting is more appropriate (e.g. boss and subordinate). However, if someone is always relying on you for help, emotional support, money, time, etc. and doesn't show appreciation or gives little of the same in return, you may want to consider if they are taking advantage of you. Sometimes some inequity in these areas can be acceptable, even normal, and relationships shouldn't be like transactions, but if you feel that someone in your life is using you in some way, this may be a red flag.
- Emotional Awareness: Everyone's different, and everyone has a different capacity when it comes to expressing and understanding emotions. However, everyone can improve in this area and show that they are trying to understand your needs and feelings. If someone consistently claims that they "aren't good with emotions" and show no willingness to develop in this area, this may be a red flag.
- Ultimatums: Does this person often use ultimatums to get what they want from you? Do you often feel pressured to say certain things, act a certain way, or give up in an

argument because you are concerned about the consequences? For example, does your boss or co-worker hold your employment and the threat of firing over your head unreasonably, for minor, resolvable workplace issues? If this happens to be the case, or if someone else you know uses ultimatums repeatedly even after you've pointed out the problem, this may be a red flag.

- Apologies: Someone's ability to give a good, meaningful apology is a strong indicator of their emotional maturity. People who cannot apologize properly or make amends in other ways demonstrate an inability to self-reflect, empathize with others, and take responsibility. If someone consistently struggles to give a thoughtful apology that shows they understand their wrongdoing and will change in the future, that can be a red flag. This is true even if they are someone 'higher' in the hierarchy than you, including bosses, parents, and older friends.

- Isolation: Manipulative people will often try to isolate others from the people in their life. It makes quite a lot of sense: if you don't have your friends and family to tell you how terrible they are, there's a greater chance you won't realize it! Be wary of people who try to monopolize your time, draw you away from your support systems, or tell you that everyone in your life doesn't 'get' you like they do. Especially in romantic or sexual relationships, this last one can be alluring. However, it can be a red flag that they want to assert control over you.

- Intuition: When it comes to red flags, the most important tool in your arsenal is intuition, or your gut feelings. In modern times, most humans have lost the ability to listen to our instincts. We are often too quick to dismiss them as irrational or paranoid. But how many times have you had a 'funny' feeling about a person or situation that turns out to be well-founded? It's quite common. Becoming more in tune with your body's physical responses to others (hair raising on your arm, an instinct to run away, a weight in your stomach or compression in your chest) will help you become more aware of potentially dangerous people – even those disguised as friends. Remember, if someone makes you feel bad constantly, you worry about seeing them, or you feel a little unnerved by what they say or do, this is a good indication that something's a bit 'off.' Trust your intuition.

- Negativity: People who bring negativity to your interactions set it off on the wrong foot every time. A tendency to focus on the negative side of things indicates a mindset that may negatively impact you. Of course, everyone has bad days where everything seems gloomy. Still, if someone is always nit-picking everything around them, bringing others down with negative feedback, or unreasonably conveying a sense that the world is against them, that may be a red flag.

- Physical Boundaries: All good relationships have well-drawn and respected physical boundaries. These boundaries will vary according to the relationship and the personalities of those involved. However, there is one golden rule: if someone feels uncomfortable about someone's physical behavior, they are within their rights to draw the line – strongly if necessary. It doesn't matter if the other person 'intended' just to be 'friendly' or just sees themselves as overly 'affectionate'; if you can't trust them to respect your boundaries, you can't trust them at all. And that's a red flag.

- Respect for You: Your coworkers and acquaintances (and even your family) don't necessarily have to like you, but they do have to respect you. People who subtly ridicule you, put you or your work down, or seem intent on changing you, don't have respect for you and your right to live your life autonomously. If someone you know is determined to see you a certain way that you don't agree with or wants to force you to do or say things, it's a sign that they don't respect you – a definite red flag.

- That Feel-Good Feeling: Do you know that feeling you get when you're on your way to visit a friend, loved one, or romantic partner, and you just can't get the smile off your face? That feeling when your body seems to glow, and you feel a pleasant sense of anticipation? That should be the goal or at least the general direction of all your relationships. Of course, you can't have this all the time in all relationships, but you can train yourself to be more aware and proactive about the ones that don't feel this way. This can help you to set up healthy boundaries, avoid traps of manipulation, and even physical, emotional, or financial abuse. To the best of your abilities, surround yourself with people who value who you are, show interest in your life, and have appropriately deep emotional connections.

Chapter 13: Becoming a Better Listener

Becoming a better listener is the best thing that you can do when you want to read people. People are not always great at communication. Meaning, they often miscommunicate their needs or wants. But if you are very careful and astute listener, you can find out all the clues that people leave around and create a more complete picture of what people are trying to say to you. By becoming a better listener, you also make people want to open up to you. They will want to talk to you more and tell you things. You will become the person that everyone wants to confide in, and then you will bear a lot of pertinent information about people.

Create an Aura of Caring

If you project that you care, people will trust you and feel at ease around you. They will be more inclined to talk to you and confess intimate things to you. Creating this image that you are a caring person involves making yourself look trustworthy and interested.

Body language is important in this endeavor. You should also lean toward the person who is talking. Hold eye contact. Nod now and then. You can cross your legs to indicate that you feel comfortable, but avoid crossing your arms as this makes you appear closed off. Try having a more open stance instead, with your chest facing the person speaking to you. Of course, always look at the speaker with a normal eye contact level to show your deference in listening.

You also want to show genuine interest. Nodding is one way to do this. Frequently murmur in an assenting or sympathetic way. You can input enough of your own words to keep the conversation going, but it is important to not talk too much. The focus needs to be on the other person.

Stop talking about yourself. As a human being, you will want to talk about yourself. It is natural. But to be a good listener, you should keep the entire conversation focused on the other person, at least while he or she is talking. Not talking about yourself or constantly trying to turn the conversation onto yourself will make you appear better listeners.

Mirroring is another way that you can make someone feel at ease around you.

Mirroring

You can set people at ease by mirroring their physical movements. You just want to copy whatever someone does during conversation. If someone leans forward, lean forward about four seconds later. If someone leans back in his seat, lean back in your seat.

Matching your breath to the same rhythm as someone else's is a subliminal form of mirroring that often will set a person at ease. The person won't even know why he feels so comfortable around you. But he will and he will open up.

It may be hard to do this if you are not close to someone. Just notice when his chest fills with air and inhale at the same time. When his nostrils inflate with exhalation, exhale as well.

Ask Questions

Get a person to talk about himself. Since people love to talk about themselves, asking lots of questions will make people happy in conversation. Keep the conversation focused on the other person and ask him plenty of questions to keep him going. For instance, if he is telling you about work, be sure to ask lots of questions about his job. Keep your questions calm and insert them at natural moments or lulls in the conversation to avoid looking like you are interrogating him.

If someone is passionate about something, definitely start asking him questions about his passion. This is a great way to get someone to open up to you. It also makes people want to talk to you. You can get to know people just by finding out what they like and then asking a few questions about it to get them talking.

Asking also is better than mind reading. If you want to understand someone, ask him what he is thinking. Ask him what he means when he says something that you don't quite understand. Don't attempt to play the mind reading game because this is how miscommunication can arise. Clear all miscommunication by asking questions instead.

Reduce Distractions

Nothing makes you look like you don't care as much as you are distracted. Put your phone away. Don't stare at the TV. Don't stare out the window or try to eavesdrop on other people. Give your full attention to the person that you are currently speaking to. Everyone that you speak to will feel valued and appreciated as a result. You will become more liked.

You will also free yourself of distractions to devote all of your energy to the conversation. This makes you a better conversationalist. You are better able to listen and retain information. You are better able to remember what is said. You can think of appropriate responses to keep the conversation from going flat or awkward.

Summarize What Was Said

After a person tells you something, it can help offer a recap to show that you were listening and make sure that you got everything understood correctly. Your summary can be brief; you don't have to regurgitate the entire conversation. But a brief recap can help both you and the other party assure that you listened well and the conversation was properly understood. It also assures the other party that you cared enough to reiterate.

Recognize What Is Unsaid

A large part of human communication is silent. What someone does not say in person is often said in other subtle ways, such as through sighs, long pauses, tear-glistening eyes, raised or lowered tone and pitch of voice, and tense body language. Notice when someone is not saying and ask if everything is OK. If the person doesn't want to talk about what he is not saying, don't press the issue. But watch his body language and eye contact to gauge what he is not telling you.

Don't Think Ahead

You may race to think ahead about what to say next. You think that you know how the conversation will go and what the person will say next, so you think that you can decide what to say ahead of time. Unfortunately, you are not a mind reader. Your predictions will often prove inaccurate. Prevent confusion or embarrassment by holding your tongue. Only decide what to say when it is your turn to speak. Then you know what was fully said and you can make an informed and suitable response.

Be Careful about Interrupting

Typically, it is wise to never interrupt. When you interrupt someone, you invalidate what he is saying. You can insult and even anger people by interrupting them. It is best to just wait your turn to speak.

However, there are times when you must speak out of turn. One good time is when the person you are speaking to begins to get overly emotional. You should interrupt politely to reassure him and tell him that he should not be so upset. Another time is when someone is talking about making a very foolish mistake. You can interrupt to offer cautionary advice. But be sure to only pick times when it is necessary to interrupt. Otherwise, avoid doing so, no matter how excited you are to jump in with what you have to say.

Determine If You Should Add Input

Sometimes, it is OK to just sit there and listen. Few people ever do this, so you will stand out as a good listener should you do this. By being silent, you allow the person you are speaking to the opportunity to unabashedly open up. He can vent and tell you all and you will absorb it all.

Other times, your input is required. People rely on for advice, for instance, or they need you to offer some words to show your interest. Wait for certain pauses in conversation when the person seems expectant. This is when you should add input.

A friendly conversation or a conversation where you are trying to get to know someone is usually a back and forth. This is when your input is required. You seem like a stick in the mud if you don't contribute to such conversations. A conversation where someone is explaining something to you or venting about his life is when your silence is required.

As a human being, you have certain social instincts. You should follow these instincts. You also know the person that you are speaking to and the nature of your conversation the best. Listen to your gut about when to speak and what to say.

Remember Things

Remembering what people say to you is a crucial part of listening. If you can reiterate what someone says to you later on, you can prove that you were listening. You can continue the conversation where it was left off if you get cut off. You can also retain important information that someone imparts to you about him- or herself.

It is easier to remember everything when you genuinely care about it. But what if you don't care? Or what if you have a lot on your mind so you have trouble retaining information in the short term? The human mind chooses to dump any information that it does not find relevant and important to your overall life. Let's face it, a lot of the conversations you have are not that relevant or important. Therefore, it is hard to remember what you hear in conversation all of the time. Shocking or really important things might stick with you, but other details quickly fade away. You can certainly improve your ability to remember conversations by using some of the following tricks.

One trick to remembering what is said to you can be to think that you will narrate this whole conversation to someone else later. While this may not be true, it tricks your mind into remembering what someone says to you better.

Another trick is to memorize important images that stand out to you in the conversation. If someone talks about what she expects from a lover, assign images to the things she says. You can assign flowers to romance, for instance. Then, you will remember a series of images better than a long string of words.

The mind is often good at remembering emotions above all else. Therefore, you should try to remember the emotional textures of the conversation. What made the speaker very sad? What made you sad? Adding emotional charges to the conversation can help you remember its main themes better.